HANNIBAL

The Ultimate Warrior: The Untold Story

by

Joseph Peebles

Copyright (c) 1994 by Joseph Peebles

Library of Congress Catalog Card Number 94-93928

ISBN 0-9644758-1-2

Hannibal, The Ultimate Warrior: The Untold Story/Joseph Peebles.

1st Edition

The Peebco Publishing House
P.O. Box 45333
St. Louis, MO 63145

Printed in the United States of America

This book has been dedicated
to my wonderful wife,
Evelyn Rice-Peebles and our son,
Joseph James Peebles.

ACKNOWLEDGMENTS

A book like this can only be the result of the contributions of many people. My first warmest thanks goes out to the God and Motherly Saint that I worship. Secondly, I am truly grateful to my wife, Evelyn, who gave me the time and long hours of assistance in writing this book. Last but not least, my deepest appreciation goes out to Dr. John L. Johnson, author of *The Black Biblical Heritage*(Winston-Derek Publishers, Inc., 1993). I thank you all.

TABLE OF CONTENTS

Chapter   Page

1.   Kingdom by the Sea   2
2.   Showtime   12
3.   Royal Blood Lines   24
4.   Treatments of Harassment   30
5.   The Men Down Under   36
6.   This Heel's for You   42
7.   Preventive Maintenance   52
8.   Fire in the Chariot House   58
9.   The Apex of Power   66
10. The Battle at Saguntum   72
11. The Race to Marseilles   82
12. Brothers in Arms   90
13. A Boxed In Situation   96
14. Another One Bites the Dust   100
15. Crossing the Alps   114
16. An Enemy from Within   122
17. Off With his Head   128
18. The Battle at Cannae   134
19. A Rude Finding   142
20. Hannibal's at the Gate   148

INTRODUCTION

The great African, Carthaginian General Hannibal Barca, was indeed instrumental in bringing forth the Euro-Renaissance. This African genius, like so many of his African compatriots, had a very high I.Q. and was widely recognized by the ancient Greeks and Romans as prudent, industrious, crafty, extremely intelligent and formidable. The illustrious Hannibal truly aroused universal attention. His contributions to world order, based upon his conception of politics, commercialism and militarism are punctiliously being studied by the intelligentsia, policy makers and social planners of the western world. Coins in the British Museum delineate him as an African who wore an ear ring.

The Carthaginians, like Hannibal, were Negroid people from Africa, who loved the sea and laterally the art of militarism. With the employment of slaves, they built great cities such as Barcelona, Spain and many profitable trading posts as far north as Great Britain. Though unequaled in both education and military strength, Hannibal and the Carthaginians, under the pen of European historians, have suffered tremendously in comparison to both Rome and Greece.

Today, many European and Western nations have credited both Rome and Greece for its renaissance or rebirth of knowledge. This is not totally accurate. During the 12th century A.D., the European Church leaders had chosen, once again, to launch a military campaign against Moslem-held Spain. The name crusade came from the Latin word crux (cross), and referred to the emblem worn by the European warriors. The Moslems (i.e., Moors, which was a popular name for Negroes all over Europe) called the Crusaders "Franks," even though they came not only from France, but by the order of the Latin Church, from all over Europe.

After the European Crusaders conquered Spain, they found a treasure in Toledo, a treasure that seems far greater than all the gold in Africa. These treasures were books left behind by the Moorish troops. The books were on subjects that were totally unfamiliar to the European and Latin scholars. The subjects were Algebra, Geometry, advanced medicine, Logic, Chemistry and Physics. Unable to read the alphabet, Latin scholars sought the assistance of Hebrew and Arab translators to help interpret Moorish words such as zero, one, two, 90 degree angle and Y and X consonants. This new found information transformed Europeans from magical and mythical thinkers to cause and effect thinkers. These Spanish Moors were Carthaginians.

The same situation existed with the war between Rome and Carthage. After winning the war against Carthage, Rome inherited more than just a nation of slaves, they inherited a culture. This culture brought along with it it's engineering, agriculture, military practices and other social treasures such as music and furniture making. Without this inherited culture, Rome, like Europe and its later renaissance, would not have fared nearly as well as its recorded history has stated.

It should be noted that the Roman army, like the French army under Napoleon Bonaparte, an Italian and first emperor of France, had many Negro generals and high ranking officers in their armies. St. Maurice, the Moor, of Aganaum, under Diocletian and Maximian Herculius, was a well-accomplished Negro general in the Roman army. The story of St. Maurice is an interesting one and it deserves inclusion within this introduction.

St. Maurice was a general in the Roman army during 287 A. D. Within this period, the western world was being jointly ruled by both Diocletian and Maximian Herculius. St. Maurice commanded a legion composed of both Negro and Italian soldiers in the Roman province of Mauritania, in upper Egypt. This was a critical time for the Roman government. The new gospel, Christianity, was spreading like wildfire. In lieu of the beatings, red-irons, and murders performed by the Roman government, the Christians were emerging from the catacombs like springtime plants. The outspoken Christian unity had become a threat to the throne of Caesar. Furthermore, German and French slaves, who were called Gauls, had joined the Christian movement and had chosen to revolt against Roman rule.

St. Maurice, along with other Roman soldiers, was summoned home to Rome and ordered to suppress these liberal movements. St. Maurice was dispatched to Aganaum, Switzerland. Upon arrival, he was stunned to learn that he and the people he was sent to suppress had something in common: they were Christians. He assembled his men and advised them not to take up arms against his brothers in Christ.

After receiving the news, Maximian assembled well over 100,000 Roman soldiers and journeyed north to Aganaum, Switzerland. Upon arrival, he ordered St. Maurice to kill the Christians. He would not. Maximian then lined up several of St. Maurice's own soldiers and had them killed before him. St. Maurice still refused to kill any Christians. Maximian continued the slaughter until St. Maurice, himself, was killed. For this, and so many other European unsung Negro heroes, all of Europe and the new world shall be forever indebted to the likes of Hannibal and other great men of color.

This story is a modern interpretation of a particular event in history. It is the untold story of Hannibal, the Ultimate Warrior.

Kingdom By The Sea

The year was 234 B.C. After the first Punic War, Carthage, Africa lost a great deal of its northern provinces to Rome, Italy. The provinces were Sicily, Corsica and Sardinia. For military and economical survival, the Carthaginian senate chose to send Hamilcar Barca to Spain to defend against continued Roman aggression. Spain was very important to both Carthage and Rome because this territory had the richest silver mines in the world.

The city of Carthage, located in north Africa, in the country of Tunisia, was by no means a poor man's town. Due to its rich Phoenician trade, Carthage had acquired a wealth far greater than any other colony in that part of the world. Stone bridges, outdoor cafes and cultivated date and palm trees were all common sobrieties of Carthage.

Many Carthaginian citizens were allowed to prosper from its merchant's trading wealth. Streetside fruit stands and fabric trading shops lined many of Carthage's urban streets. Schools and advanced universities were also part of Carthaginian life. Many of its citizens were well learned in politics, music, poetry, religion, botany, zoology, mathematics, engineering, chemistry, law, anatomy, geometry and philosophy.

As the August sun over the city burned with an immense intensity, the sweltering, midday heat brought most life to a crawl inside this kingdom by the sea. In contrast, to the slow paced rhythmic movement, the east side of the city was alive with the clamor of arguing senators inside the domed senate building. The gyrations and physical movements of the senators suggested a passionate debate on an issue of great importance.

"I say we go to war, take back Sicily and cancel all war indemnity payments," shouted a Carthaginian senator. "We are just as powerful as Rome, if not more!"

"I even hear that the Romans are taxing the citizens three talents a year," shouted another senator. "Those are our tax revenues."

"This is barbaric," shouted another senator. "We must stop Roman aggression or they'll be here in Carthage next!"

A loud blast from the senate trumpeter interrupted the chamber debate.

"All rise for his majesty, the King," announced the bailiff.

All members present rose to their feet as the Carthaginian King made his entrance into the chamber. He was escorted by two muscular guards. The guards' towering appearance, with their sculptured, coal-black bodies, signaled bad news to any would-be dissident.

The King possessed an appearance of surefooted nobility. His purple garment, engraved with gold trim, hung loosely and billowed behind him like the sails of a ship as he strode majestically toward his seat of honor. After he took his seat at his throne, he signaled to the bailiff with a nod of his head.

"You all may be seated," the bailiff said to the senators. He then unrolled a scroll and read it before the King. "Your majesty, this senate has before you today a second declaration of war against Rome. The objective of this war is to take back the provinces of Sicily, Corsica and Sardinia and place them back into African domain."

"It is my understanding that neither our military nor our economy has fully recovered from the first war," said the King. "Furthermore, according to our crop forecaster, our autumn harvests are going to be extremely low for the next two years. How do we feed and finance such a campaign?"

"We go and take Spain," announced Hamilcar Barca as he took center stage on the senate floor.

"Why Spain?" asked the King.

"Because Spain has the richest silver mines in the world," answered Hamilcar Barca. "I've calculated that after three years of successful mining, we can easily make enough swords, shields and breast plates to equip fifty thousand men for battle."

"And what about our war agreement with Rome?" asked the King.

Hamilcar Barca folded his arms and answered with confidence:

"The Romans wouldn't dare fight us in Spain. The bulk of their army and navy is protecting the islands and their portion of the purple dye trade routes. Furthermore, Spain has the best autumn harvest in this part of the world. Our slaves, who would be mining the silver mines, would remain healthy well into the early part of the spring. The logistics are perfect."

"I don't think that this is a good idea," responded a standing senate member. "I say let Romans be Romans and Carthaginians be Carthaginians. As long as Rome stays on their side of the Mediterranean, I vote that we leave the war issue alone and keep current on our war payments."

Hamilcar Barca turned toward the standing senate member and said:

"Sheik Massinissa, isn't it true that you are the wealthiest slave trader in all of Africa?"

"Yes," he answered proudly.

"And isn't it also true that you have a secret trade agreement with the Romans?"

Sheik Massinissa didn't answer. He simply stared dumbly at Barca.

"Well?" Barca demanded.

"Yes, but only in return for Roman silver and robe wear," concluded Sheik Massinissa.

Barca then turned toward the King and said:

"I vote that before we go to war against the Romans, we take a permanent interest in Spain's mineral rich fields and afterward, we march in and burn Rome."

Cheers rang throughout the senate chamber. Barca was honored with a standing ovation.

"Silence in the chamber," ordered the bailiff. "Silence in the chamber!"

"Senators, let us put this issue to vote," said the King. "All those in favor of Carthage taking Spain, raise your hand."

The majority of the senators voted in favor of war.

"All of those opposed," asked the King.

Only a few voted against the issue.

"Then it is settled," concluded the King. "We go to war against Spain and after three years of successful mining, only then will I give my blessing on war against Rome. Barca, Massissina, I would like to see both of you in my chambers immediately. This session is adjourned."

The King's chamber was a stern facade of marble arches and golden columns. Its fortress-like interior was embellished with artwork of olive groves and men in chariots. Perched above the entrance was a huge portrait of the king. The portrait was framed with gleaming wood and accented with the gold of Africa. Also, accented with the gold of Africa was his large ebony throne. Carved into the wood of the throne were the ancestors of his royal lineage.

After both Barca and Massinissa had entered the King's chamber, the King took his seat at his throne and said to the bailiff:

"You are dismissed. Thank you." He then said to Barca and Massinissa: "Please be seated, my brothers."

After both men had taken their seat at the King's round table, the King's two military escort stood behind the King.

"Now, let us discuss this issue," said the King. "Sheik Massinissa, why have you violated our ordinance of slave trading with the Romans?"

"My Kingship, Hamilcar Barca does not speak the entire truth," Sheik Massinissa said nervously. "He is a man full of envy."

"Why should I envy you, Massinissa," Barca asked him. "I am the general in charge of the entire Carthaginian Army. It is through my efforts, via war, that you have become a very rich man. I clearly do not understand your defense before this great King. Would you like another rebuttal?"

"My Kingship, I confess, I have sold a few slaves to some Roman auctioneers but not many," explained Sheik Massinissa.

"I would call fifteen thousand slaves a substantial amount," Barca interrupted. He then stood before the king and said, "My kingship, must we continue with this? We have an entire nation to conquer. May we resolve this issue so that we can move onto the business of Spain?"

"Yes, Barca, we can," agreed the King. "Sheik Massinissa, it doesn't matter whether you sold one slave or one thousand, you knowingly disobeyed this land's law. Therefore, all of your male slaves 16 years of age and older will go to Spain with Barca to work the silver mines. The women and children 15 years of age and younger will become the property of the Carthaginian government. They will work the public fields as indentured servants. You may keep your money but you are hereby ordered by this government never to trade another slave on this great continent of Africa. If you violate this order, you shall receive a punishment far worse than death. Do we understand one another?"

"Yes, my Kingship," Massinissa said disappointedly.

"Good! You are now dismissed," finished the King. "You are to report to the Sergeant of Arms. Confiscation is to begin immediately."

2

Showtime

And so the great quest was on. After four months of training and preparation, Hamilcar Barca was off to Spain. Spain was approximately one day of travel from Carthage. Their first confrontation came within 12 hours of sailing. It was against Jacko, the Illyrian pirate.

Dressed in battle armor and draped in his customary purple Carthaginian cape, Hamilcar Barca stood on the bridge of his vessel appreciating the warm winter daylight. He was then rapidly approached by the ship's drum communication officer.

"Sir, an Illyrian pirate ship has been spotted off our left v-wing assembly," the officer said breathing heavily.

"How far away is it," asked Barca.

The drum communication officer asked the question by drum beats to the point ship. After a few seconds, he received a response by drum beats from the point ship. He then said to Barca:

"It is five miles away, sir."

"Has it spotted us yet?" Barca asked the drum communication officer.

Again, the drummer asked the question via drum beats to the point ship. He received a response.

"Yes it has. It is headed toward our left wing destroyer."

Barca called for his son-in-law and second in command:

"Hasdrubal?"

"Sir," answered Hasdrubal.

"Who is in charge of our left wing destroyer?" he asked.

"Your son, Hannibal," answered Hasdrubal.

"Tell him to prepare for battle," said Barca. "An enemy ship is headed in his direction."

Featured center stage in the ship's cargo bay, in the midst of cheering Carthaginian soldiers, was Hannibal Barca and two full-grown Brahma Bulls. Holding both bulls by their reins, Hannibal was competing against them in a true test of strength.

Hannibal was a man of great muscular stature. He stood well over six feet in height and weighed close to two hundred pounds. His skin was golden bronze in color. Below a v-shaped torso were his tree trunk-like legs. They were solidly planted as he competed against the bulls in a tug-of-war contest. Fastened behind his handsome, bronzed face were his woolly locks of African hair.

As he held onto the reins, the massive muscles in his large arms flexed and bulged with bursting momentum. Periodically, the bulls would receive a lashing from the ring master's whip that signified more pulling action. Finally, after several minutes of competition, the reins snapped in two. Hannibal fell backward and was caught by two Carthaginian soldiers. He was then approached by his drum communication officer.

"Sir, I have an urgent message from your father," said the drummer.

"Well, speak up," Hannibal said between breaths.

"You are to prepare for battle against Jacko, the Pirate. He is headed directly toward us."

"Great," Hannibal said excitedly. "Let's go boys. It's showtime!" He then scrambled up two flights of stairs and took a commanding position on the bridge. He gave the order. "Forward all rudders, lower all masts and give me ramming speed."

Down below, in the ship's galley, the slaves were being chained into their rowing position. After the shackles were firmly fastened around their right ankles, the oars were set in the ready position. The total chained-seating assembly consisted of 100 slaves starboard and 100 slaves port side.

Jacko's ship was sleek, thin and fast. Jacko, himself, was a man of a wild and risque appearance. His long hair draped wildly over his head. His teeth were bad and his body lacked a bath. Physically, he too, was a man of great muscular stature and he towered well over seven feet in height.

Standing on his bridge, he was approached by his lookout officer.

"Sir, I believe that one of the Carthaginian vessels has positioned itself for confrontation."

"Good! Let's take our first lamb," Jacko said in his deep, bass-like voice. "Load all catapults and give me a hard left rudder.

Jacko's men scrambled to place moist mortar in the spoons of their catapults. They then stood in the ready position with lit torches in their hands.

"On my command, light the mortar," Jacko said.

As Jacko's ship moved closer toward Hannibal's vessel, Hannibal took a firm control of his crew.

"Hanno," Hannibal called out.

"Sir," answered Hanno, Hannibal's chief in-command.

"Are we ready?"

"Ready and willing," Hanno answered.

"Good! Give me a beat," Hannibal commanded to Hanno.

"You heard the man. Let's get busy. Give me a beat," Hanno said to the drummer below. "Give me two-thirds ramming speed."

The muscular, coal-black, shirtless drummer set the drum beat at two-thirds. He then began the cadence.

"Heave!"

"Hooooo," responded the slaves as they began to row.

"Heave, humpers!"

"Hooooo!

"Heave!"

"Hooooo!"

"Heave, humpers!"

"Hooooo!

"Light the mortar," ordered Jacko.

"Archers, take aim," Hannibal ordered.

"Fire," shouted Jacko.

"Fire," shouted Hannibal.

Both arrows and burning mortar crossed the sky simultaneously. Most of the mortar missed Hannibal's ship. Hannibal's archers struck several of Jacko's men. Jacko's wounded fell overboard into the Mediterranean.

"Reload," Jacko ordered to his men.

The crew scrambled to place more mortar into the spoons of the catapults.

"Fire all arrows at will," Hannibal commanded to his archers.

"Fire," Jacko shouted to his men.

The incoming mortar rained down heavily onto Hannibal's deck like flaming meteorites. As the fire continued to spread, several of his men were engulfed by the flames. To extinguish themselves, they dove into the Mediterranean Sea.

"Fire on deck! Fire on deck," shouted a Carthaginian soldier.

"Give me more ramming speed," Hannibal shouted forcefully!

"More ramming speed," Hanno ordered to the drummer below.

"Heave," the drummer said as he increased his drum rhythm.

"Hooooo," shouted the slaves.

"Faster," shouted the drummer.

"Hooooo!"

Jacko's ship swiftly positioned itself next to Hannibal's vessel.

"Forward all rudders and prepare to fasten ourselves to the Carthaginian ship," Jacko said as he slid down a mast onto his lower deck.

Both ships collided. The earth quake collision caused both ships to loose men over the sides.

"Javelin throwers, present arms," Hannibal ordered.

With their swords in their hands, several dozen of Jacko's men leaped onto Hannibal's flaming deck.

"Javelin throwers, release arms," Hannibal commanded.

The javelin throwers released their spears at Jacko's intruding highjackers. Many of Jacko's men were struck by the spears. With loud screams, several wounded fell overboard into the sea.

Jacko, with his sword in his hand, led another group of men in a charge against the Carthaginians. Like a track and field long jumper, Jacko made a running leap onto Hannibal's flaming deck.

Hannibal immediately recognized Jacko. He withdrew his sword and swung down a rope toward Jacko. On the flaming deck, with hundreds of battling soldiers around them, Hannibal and Jacko engaged in a sword fight.

Rapidly advancing from the rear of Hannibal's vessel was another Carthaginian war ship. Its crew, once they were within striking range, released their arrows, via bows, at Jacko's ship.

"Heave," shouted the galley drummer of the second Carthaginian war ship.

"Hooooo," shouted the rowing slaves of the second ship.

"Faster, humpers!"

"Hooooo!"

The second war ship slammed into Jacko's ship. The slammed momentum vibrated through both Hannibal's and Jacko's ships. As the second war ship continued to move forward, it created a large hole in Jacko's super structure. Sea water rushed into Jacko's galley section. His chained slaves scrambled to break free from their shackles. They were both panicky and unsuccessful.

Jacko quickly realized that his ship was going under. Frenzied, he let go a scream and charged toward Hannibal. Both men wrestled on the flaming deck. Minutes later, with Jacko on top of Hannibal, the fight ended. Both men lay still. Hannibal, with very little physical effort, shoved Jacko aside and withdrew his sword from Jacko's stomach. Jacko was dead.

Shortly there afterward, peace was restored to Hannibal's ship. The fires were extinguished and Jacko's body, along with the rest of his crew, was either thrown or forced to jump overboard.

From the bridge of the second Carthaginian war ship, Hannibal was asked by the ship's Captain:

"Hannibal, how do you feel?"

"Like a winner," Hannibal responded with a smile. He then turned and called for his assistant, "Hanno?"

"Sir," answered Hanno.

"Raise the masts, reward the slaves with plenty of food and fresh water and forward all

rudders.   We're off to Spain," Hannibal said
proudly.

"Yes sir!"

3

Royal Blood Lines

The southeastern shore of Spain required a great deal of excavating before landing. The tall treelined shore made the mainland difficult to reach by ship. The relationship between beach and water also offered very little in hospitality. Huge boulders and low waters were the signatures of New Carthage, Spain.

Hamilcar Barca stood on his starboard bow and overlooked Spain's shoreline. After he assessed the situation carefully, he called for his second in command:

"Hasdrubal?"

"Sir," he answered.

"I want the right wing assembly to go ashore first. The left wing assembly will remain in the harbor until the right wing has cleared the way onto the beaches."

"Yes sir."

After a tricky and dangerous landing, the slaves were sent to form a human assembly line. They passed boxes of supplies and grain from the cargo ship onto the beach. As the evening wore on, they continued to work by torch light. Around midnight, the slaves had built a ramp and had unloaded the chariots, oxen and horses from their storage bins.

All was quiet as the morning dawn approached. Tents, animals and supplies were all aligned in an orderly fashion and the slaves were fast asleep.

Hannibal stood at the entrance of his tent. He stretched his arms and took a deep breath of the early morning air. He then took the leash of his pet lion, Leo and both went for a stroll along the beach. He was joined by his father, Hamilcar Barca.

"Good morning, my son."

"Good morning, my father."

"Did you rest well," asked Hamilcar Barca.

"Yes sir, I did and yourself?"

"Fine, thank you. How's Leo?"

"Lion-like as ever," answered Hannibal.

"Good. You performed brilliantly against Jacko, the pirate yesterday. Was he much trouble for you?"

"Of course not," Hannibal answered. "It was child's play."

"My son, in order to shape your great future, you must know your great past. The Barca family is truly from royal blood lines. Many centuries ago, our people lived in the land of Canaan. Canaan, himself, was the fourth son of Ham, the youngest son of Noah. Canaan's oldest son, Sidon, is our ancestral father. The land of Canaan was a peaceful place for our people until

Joshua Ben Nun led the Israelites across the Jordan River and beyond the walls of Jericho. Rather than share the land with the Israelites, some of our people, being the great Phoenician merchants that we were, had chosen to come to a land that was both fertile and far, far away from the intruders. That land was Carthage, Africa. Your great grandfather, who was also a Barca and a direct descendent of the Phoenician king, had promised to never allow another foreign nation to force our people from their homes. He became the trainer and leader of the Carthaginian Army. It was he who made Corsica, Sardinia and Sicily African colonies."

"Where was his body laid to rest," asked Hannibal.

"In Barcelona, Sicily," Barca answered. "So you see, we do have a permanent interest in those three islands and if Baal is willing, we will get them back."

"My father, I swear to you by the blood of our royal ancestors, I will do all I can to retrieve our islands from those mean-spirited Romans."

"Good, I do like your attitude," said Hamilcar Barca. "Today, we are heading north to Saguntum to begin our first mining operation."

"Are we going to secure the beaches and form communications and supply lines along the way?"

"Yes, we are. I am taking Hasdrubal north with me to engineer the mining operations. I would like for you to secure the beaches and supply routes. We shall make this port city our very first colony. I do expect good relations with the locals."

"Yes sir. And what shall we call this new port city," Hannibal asked.

"Let's name it after our beloved Carthage. We shall name it Cartagena."

4

Treatments of Harassment

Rome was a city of both legend and fantasy. It was also a city of ideals that lent itself to the ways of opulence, decadence and gaiety. By design, only the rich and politically astute were allowed to live within the inner walls of the city. These people were Latins. Latins had either a deep base olive skin tone or a darkish beige complexion.

Outside the city, beyond its great wall, were people of lesser privileges. They were not Latins; they were Ligurians. Ligurians were said to be tough, hairy and wild natured. Their small, grass-roofed dwellings were scattered throughout the country side in an array of tribal villages. Further to the north of Rome were the Lombards. They were farmers and wine makers.

Many of the city's paintings and architecture reflected the imperial attitudes of the Latins (i.e., Romans). Three different marbles were used for their floor patterns. The unforgettable atmosphere also gave way to huge buildings, large, leisurely amphitheaters and oversized seated athletic playing fields.

Late into the night, the sounds of laughter and merry making could be heard within her walls. The constant clattering of chariot wheels was also a familiar sound of the city. The challenges and wagers of Rome's youth was another constant event. On this particular day, such an event was the case.

On the playing field where the Roman Coliseum would later be built, the evening's entertainment was getting underway. The evening's event was the sparing of two champion gladiators.

"In this corner, we have Titus, the champion of the Gauls," shouted the stadium announcers.

Titus was a strong and muscular, blonde-haired man from northern Europe. As he ran out onto the playing field, he was greeted with boos and jeers.

"And in this corner we have Bruno, the Black Italian," the announcer shouted with excitement.

Bruno was a cross between a hairy Ligurian and an African. He too, was a tall and muscular man. As he ran out onto the playing field, he was welcomed with cheers and honors of applause. He then stomped his way toward the center of the playing field twirling his spiked ball and chain. After he approached Titus, he spat at him.

Seated together, high in the choice stadium box seats, was the Roman Emperor Quintus Fabius Maximus and his chief military general, Publius Cornelius Scipio. Both men were Latins and both men were in their early fifties.

"Cornelius, I'll bet you fifteen talents that Bruno defeats Titus in three rounds," said Fabius Maximus.

"Make it twenty, Fabius and we have a deal," said Cornelius Scipio.

"You're on."

The gladiators squared off for battle in the middle of the field. After they presented arms, they immediately went to blows.

"Have you heard that the Africans from Carthage have invaded Spain," Fabius asked Cornelius.

"In fact I have," answered Cornelius. "What do you suspect?"

"I don't know. I understand that they are excavating the silver mines just south of the Ebro River. They have also set up several trading posts throughout Spain."

"Should we intervene," Cornelius asked.

The crowd chanted loudly for Bruno.

"No," Fabius said over the loud chants. "Why buy the cow when you can get the milk free. As long as they remain current on their war indemnity payments, let them mine."

"I don't know about this one, Fabius," said Cornelius. "I really believe that we should be monitoring their movements and developments in Spain. After all, they are Carthaginians and they shouldn't be taken lightly."

The crowd released an ah as Titus drew blood, with his sword, from Bruno's arm. Bruno kicked Titus back with a drop kick. The crowd responded with cheers and excitement.

"I'm sure you're right, Cornelius," said Fabius. "But at this particular time, I don't want a full scale war with Carthage. I'll send a declaration to the Carthaginian government demanding that their army remains south of the Ebro River. I'll also send your brother Cnaeus, along with two thousand troops, to Spain to enforce the declaration and to offer treatments of harassment."

"And if they don't obey?"

"You will have my permission to go to war."

"Good," Cornelius responded.

The stadium crowd began to cheer wildly. Bruno had defeated Titus. Bruno stood over Titus's badly mangled body, spat and then pronounced victory over his opponent.

Cornelius settled back in his seat, folded his arms and said:

"Game's over; you lose. It took Bruno four rounds to win."

5

The Men Down Under

The heavy downpour of rain over the Saguntum mining camp created a thick curtain of water. The thunderous skies were illuminated with bright flashes of lightning. Electricity filled the air as Hasdrubal took shelter beneath the silver mine entrance. Behind him, slaves hauled huge chunks of silver ore, through the vertical flood of water, out of the mine. He was then joined by a Carthaginian mining officer.

"How many measures of silver are we mining on a daily basis," asked the mining officer.

"I'd estimate about 3,000 to 4,000 measures per day, if not more," Hasdrubal said as he examined a raw piece of silver. He then said:

"This is good quality silver. There are very few other metals mixed in."

Suddenly, there came a crashing noise deep within the mine. Slaves screamed and ran for their lives as part of the mine collapsed. One support beam had lost its strength due to the shaking and thundering storm above.

Below, deep within the mine shaft, slaves had attempted to climb the ladder out of the silver pit. The trembling ground, along with the weight of too many men on the same ladder, had caused the two-story ladder to collapse. The men at the top of the ladder had fallen to their death into a dark and bottomless pit. Screams echoed out as they fell.

Heavy rain water had worked its way into the mine. Mud rapidly formed. Several men lost their footing and were caught up in a mud slide. Again, screams rang out as the men were lead down, in a water slide fashion, into a dark and bottomless pit.

The main ceiling beam finally lost it strength and snapped in two. The entire earth-covered ceiling collapsed and sealed off the mine's main entrance. Once the debris settled, the rain stopped.

Hasdrubal managed to crawl his way out of the muddy debris. He then signaled for help:

"Over here, we are over here," he shouted.

Several Carthaginian soldiers rushed over toward the mine entrance and pulled Hasdrubal, along with several other men, out from under the debris.

"How many men are still trapped inside," asked another Carthaginian mining officer.

"At least two hundred," Hasdrubal answered between coughs.

"I want you to get me ten oxen," said Hasdrubal. "We are going to plow our way through the entrance to allow additional oxygen to flow into the shaft."

"Yes sir, but aren't most of the men in the mine slaves," asked the mining officer.

Hasdrubal stared at him coldly and said:

"What difference does it make? They are men, aren't they? We are not that kind of people. Now get me those oxen, pronto!"

"Yes sir," answered the mining officer. He mounted his horse and swiftly rode off.

As dusk approached, the skies cleared and the promise of the rainbow unfolded above the mining camp. Riding out of the rainbow-lit horizon was Hamilcar Barca, the mining officer and several hundred cavalrymen on horseback. They rushed toward the silver mines entrance. Once they reached the entrance, they, along with other Carthaginian soldiers and slaves, hauled away mud and huge rocks. Shortly afterward, the oxen appeared.

A sharp-pointed battering ram was tied between two oxen. The oxen were driven forward into the newly formed earthen wall of the mine. Penetration was slow but sure.

"Shhhhh, I hear something," one of the entrapped slaves said in the midst of darkness.

"What is it," asked another slave.

"It sounds like a rescue team," said the first slave.

The two entrapped slaves were joined by the other surviving members. Then there came a ray of daylight. This brought hope to the survivors below. Shortly there afterward, a crashing sound was heard above. The oxen had made their way through the collapsed wall. The survivors rejoiced with cheers.

Hasdrubal was the first to crawl through the opening. He then asked:

"Is everyone all right?"

"Those present are," answered a mine worker. "We've lost quite a few people."

Hasdrubal threw a rope down into the shaft. He advised them below:

"Here, catch. Each one, help one."

Hasdrubal was joined by Hamilcar Barca. Together, they tightly tied the rope around a large boulder. Afterward, they crawled out and strolled over toward Barca's horse.

"I do thank you for helping me with this rescue mission," Hasdrubal said to Barca.

"Think nothing of it, my brother," Barca said as he mounted his horse. "Long live Carthage?"

"Yes, long live Carthage," Hasdrubal responded.

Barca returned to his camp.

6

This Heel's For You

The lower Ebro River Valley in northern Spain, just east of the Carthaginian trading town of Tortosa, offered an ocean view of heavenly proportions. Century old Camphor trees and flickering ocean waters were rarities for this part of Spain. Warm and rich greenery also added to the mise-en-scene. As the jewel-like beaches courted one's emotions, it gave no hint of the conflict ahead.

Overlooking the valley, a Carthaginian scout spotted the Roman army on the north side of the river. The scout mounted his horse and swiftly rode into Hannibal's camp. He dismounted his horse and said to Hannibal:

"Sir, I have just spotted a large infantry unit of Roman soldiers in the lower Ebro River Valley."

"How many soldiers," Hannibal asked.

"Approximately two thousand foot soldiers, five hundred cavalry men and two thousand chariot drivers," answered the scout.

"Great," Hannibal said. "Send a message to my father via drum. We have our fist confrontation with Rome."

The Roman army was led by Lt. General Cnaeus Scipio. As they approached the river, Lt. General Scipio raised his hand. He signaled for the entire infantry unit to halt. He was then joined by his cavalry master.

"Cnaeus, at what point do we strike, on the north or the south side of the river," asked the cavalry master.

"Our orders are to inspect the Carthaginian camp and to advise them to remain south of the Ebro River," Lt. General Scipio answered.

"What if they refuse?"

"Then we shall physically enforce the law."

"Good. I'll give the order," said the cavalry master. He then retreated toward the cavalry unit and said: "Load the rafts. We're crossing the river."

Charging down toward the river was Hannibal and the Carthaginian army. Hannibal led the charge on horseback. He brought his horse to a skidding stop in front of the Roman army and said:
"So, what brings the Roman army to Spain?"

"We are here to inspect your mining efforts," Lt. General Scipio said as he and his horse stood mid way in the river.

"We have no agreement with Rome concerning Spain," Hannibal said.

"One has been sent to your government in Carthage," said Lt. General Scipio. "We are requesting that you remain south of this river."

"Sorry, we don't take request. What is your name," Hannibal asked him.

"I am Lt. General Cnaeus Scipio."

"Well Lt. General Scipio, you are not crossing this river."

Lt. General Scipio assessed the situation briefly and retreated toward his cavalry master.

"Well, what do we do now," asked the Cavalry master.

Scipio compared the size of his army to that of the Carthaginians. He then said to his cavalry master:

"We're Romans. We're going ashore."

"We are also in a poor strategic position, here in the middle of this river," said the cavalry master. "There is nowhere to retreat if the battle goes against us."

"I know. So let's go forward," said Lt. General Scipio. He then turned toward Hannibal and said: "Sir, we are coming ashore.".

"It's your funeral," Hannibal said.

"Forward, march," Lt. General Scipio commanded to his troops.

Hannibal turned toward his archers and said:

"Ready, aim, fire!"

"Charge," shouted Lt. General Scipio.

The members of the Roman army jumped for their rafts and rushed forward toward the Carthaginian army. They protected themselves with their shields as the Carthaginian arrows honed in on them.

"Second division, fire at will," Hannibal commanded.

The Carthaginian second division fired their arrows at the Roman army. As the Romans continued to rush forward, many fell prey to the Carthaginian arrows.

"Forward, charge," Hannibal shouted as he led his troops into the river against the Romans.

Both armies met and fought mid way in the river.

Toward Hannibal's rear, four hundred additional Carthaginian soldiers ran and slid down a mountainous hill side to help in the waterfront battle. Swiftly moving down river were two hundred Carthaginian charioteers. Hamilcar Barca's chariot, driven by Hanno, led the backup charge. Barca rode as Hanno's passenger.

As Barca's chariot approached the heart of the battle, he dove out of his chariot and onto two Roman soldiers. After he defeated them, he withdrew his sword and defeated two more Roman soldiers.

After he defended himself against three Carthaginian soldiers, Lt. General Scipio retreated to a Roman Chariot. He reviewed his situation.

After he realized that he was losing the battle, he gave the order to his troops:

"Retreat to the north side of the river, now!"

Lt. General Scipio started this chariot and led the retreat along the Ebro River. As he drove past Hannibal, he retrieved a javelin from the water and threw it at Hannibal. He missed.

Hannibal became infuriated by this. In waist-high water, he rushed forward toward Scipio. Scipio started his chariot and sped away from Hannibal.

"Hanno, bring me your chariot," Hannibal shouted.

Hanno tossed two Roman soldiers aside and climbed into the Golden chariot. He then rode toward Hannibal. Without slowing, Hannibal ran along beside the chariot and dove on.

"Catch that chariot," Hannibal said to Hanno.

"Yes sir," said Hanno. He cracked his whip. The horses immediately went into hot pursuit of Scipio's high speed chariot.

Soon, both chariots were traveling side by side. Together, they sped dangerously around a narrow curve. After both chariots cleared the curve, Hannibal dove from his chariot and onto Scipio's chariot. After he landed, he lost his footing and slid toward the rear of the chariot. With his feet dragging the surface, Hannibal held onto Scipio's chariot tail gate assembly.

Scipio, with the reins in one hand and a whip in the other, turned sideways and attempted to strike Hannibal with his whip. Hannibal avoided every lash.

At the end of the road was a bluff that overlooked the river. Due to the uncontrollable high speed of the chariot, the horses were unable to adjust to the sharp curve in the road. As the horses rounded the curve, the right side chariot wheel rolled off its axle. Both chariot and horses tumbled several times before it rolled over the cliff.

As both men tumbled over the edge, Hannibal managed to secure a grip on an outgrown tree root that had grown out of the cliff. Lt. General Scipio tumbled over Hannibal and managed to grab hold of Hannibal's left ankle. As both men dangled over the cliff, their eyes met. Lt. General Scipio said to Hannibal:

"I know who you are. You are General Barca's son, Hannibal."

"Yes, I am and until we meet again, this heel's for you."

Hannibal kicked Lt. General Scipio free from his ankle. Scipio fell aimlessly downward and splashed hard into the river below. Hannibal watched unemotionally as Scipio drifted swiftly out to sea.

7

Preventive Maintenance

The leisurely atmosphere within the Roman senate was perfect for the day's agenda. Topics for discussion were the newly installed sewer systems, new construction on public showers and the addressing of neighborly disputes. Boringly observing the discussions and seated together at the head of the senate chamber was the Roman Emperor Quintus Fabius Maximus and Rome's chief military officer, Cornelius Scipio.

Suddenly, the doors of the senate chamber were shoved open. In walked Lt. General Cnaeus Scipio. His attire was torn and dirty. A hush fell over the senate chamber.

Cornelius stood up and looked at his brother with speechless amazement. Cnaeus stopped before both Cornelius and Fabius and saluted both men.

"Well," Fabius asked of Cnaeus.

"Well, we lost. We lost an entire infantry and cavalry unit to the Carthaginian army," Cnaeus answered.

Quiet chatter among the senators filled the chamber.

"Silence in the chamber," Fabius ordered angrily. He then turned toward Cornelius and said: "You said your brother would be competent against a small Carthaginian army."

"Fabius, it was not a small Carthaginian army," Cnaeus interrupted. "They have a unit of forty thousand plus. The Spaniards have informed me that the Carthaginians are making swords and body armor to return to war against us."

"Who is in charge of the Carthaginian army," Cornelius asked him.

"General Barca," answered Cnaeus. "He is joined by his son, Hannibal. Together, they have built a major city in honor of the Barca family. The city is called Barcelona, Spain."

Chatter again filled the senate chamber.

"Silence," shouted Fabius. "If General Barca is in Spain preparing for war, then we must do likewise."

"Barca is a well-seasoned commander," said Cornelius. "He has defeated us in both Syracuse and Drepana. He is lightning swift when it involves an offensive attack."

"So what are you suggesting, Cornelius," asked Fabius. "Do we leave the Carthaginians alone in Spain?"

"No," answered Cornelius. "I am suggesting that we eliminate General Barca. You see, if the Carthaginian army is forty thousand strong, under Barca's command, we will surely lose seventy thousand in our efforts to defeat him. We learned this in the first Punic War against the

Africans from Carthage. Without Barca, the Carthaginians are totally useless."

"For your sake, Cornelius, I hope you're right," said Fabius. He then turned toward the senate members to get a census. "Are there any senators among us today in opposition to what has been proposed?"

"Fabius, will this assassination launch us into a costly war with Carthage," asked a Roman Senator.

"Without General Barca, who within the Carthaginian army is strong enough to lead them into war against us," Fabius asked the senator.

"His son, Hannibal," answered Cnaeus. "He is daring, strong and adventurous."

"His son is only a man in his early thirties," Cornelius said to Cnaeus. "He is too inexperienced to beat even yourself."

"He already has," said Cnaeus. "It is because of him that I am standing before you today in shame."

"Consider this preventive maintenance. Eliminate only the father," said Fabius. "I don't want a costly war with Carthage. This session is adjourned. It is time for my massage." He then closed the session with a tap from his mallet.

8

Fire in the Chariot House

The victory of the Carthaginians first scrimmage against the Romans was celebrated in a rambunctious manner underneath a red evening sky. Nymphs and tambourines entertained hundreds of red-eyed, sword-waving soldiers as they danced, drank and made merry with the local Spanish girls.

"Hey, look what has just arrived," shouted a Carthaginian soldier. "Fresh beer from Egypt." He unveiled, under a covered wagon, several wooden kegs of beer.

Shortly after that, all the campsite members sang and clapped to this song:

"Long live Carthage, home of the champions to be. Where the oceans meet the skies there is a home for me."

"Long live Carthage, home of the champions to be. Where the oceans meet the skies there is a home for me."

Both Hamilcar Barca and his son-in-law, Hasdrubal, were seated together for dinner. Their meal was served underneath a tent-covered area, by a well-mannered servant. They were soon joined by Hannibal and his assistant, Hanno.

"This first victory was very important for our troop's morale," said Hasdrubal.

"Especially since this is, for many of them, their first time away from home," Hannibal said as he took his place at the dinner table.

"Yes indeed," said Hamilcar. "I suspect that things will continue to heat up between us and Rome. Hasdrubal, how are the mining operations coming along?"

"On a daily basis, our blacksmiths are mass producing five hundred swords, three hundred pieces of body armor and one thousand metal tips for our arrows and javelins."

"And our tailors," Hamilcar asked Hasdrubal.

"Onsite, the tailors are mass-producing twenty pairs of covered sandals in each size, fifty pairs of pants, in small medium and large and also with the military shirts."

"Wonderful. Wars are won based upon logistics, not troop size," said Hamilcar. "Hannibal, are the men physically and emotionally ready for battle."

"Yes, sir," Hannibal answered. "They are willing and ready."

"Good! I'm ready to go," said Hamilcar. "Any day now, our messenger should arrive with a go-ahead message from Carthage to march on Rome."

"Here is to victory," Hasdrubal said as he made a toast.

"To victory," toasted all four seated.

Hidden behind the horse stables were four Spaniards with lit torches. Unnoticeably, they crept up toward the rear entrance door. One crawled in through a window, tipped over toward the double doors, opened it and signaled for the other three to come in. They immediately rushed in and holding two flint stones, one of the men struck a spark and lit his torch. Afterward, he shared his flame with the other three. The horses reacted nervously to the smell of smoke. The Spaniards then threw their torches on the hay stacks and scrambled out the front entrance.

Walking toward the horse stables was a sentry on guard duty. He heard the nervousness of the horses and ran toward the stables.

Armed with a bow and arrow and hidden high within a tree top was another Spaniard. He calmly watched everything from a distance as the fire traveled rapidly throughout the stables.

"Fire in the chariot house! Fire in the chariot house," shouted the sentry.

One of the Spaniards withdrew his sword and aimed it at the sentry.

"Let him be," said one of the Spaniards. "Let's get out of here."

Hamilcar, Hannibal, Hasdrubal, Hanno and other Carthaginian soldiers rushed toward the burning horse stables.

The tree top Spaniard took aim at Hamilcar Barca. He then released the infamous arrow. The arrow stuck Hamilcar Barca in the chest. In great pain, he fell toward the ground.

As Hannibal and Hasdrubal stopped to help Hamilcar Barca, a senior medical officer rushed over toward Barca. As he stood over Hamilcar, the doctor caught an arrow in his back. Painfully, he slumped over Hamilcar.

Hannibal gently laid the doctor on his side. He then visually scanned the outside perimeter of the campsite. He spotted another arrow as it flew from the tree top. He, along with several other soldiers, rushed over toward the tree.

Barca coughed up blood. He then pulled Hasdrubal close to and said:

"My life is quickly coming to an end. I want you and Hannibal to continue the fight against Rome. The two of you must restore Carthage to its original glory and sovereignty."

Hannibal rushed to his father's side. With tears in his eyes, he stroked his father's gray beard and said:

"My father, on this autumn day, I promise you that I will indeed conquer Italy and that includes Rome."

"Hannibal, I want you to always be courageous and brave," he said in his dying breath. "I also want the story of Carthage properly passed down through the generation and more important, long live Carthage."

"Long live Carthage," Hannibal said to his father.

He then closed his eyes and died in Hannibal arms.

9

The Apex of Power

Hundreds of thousands of mourners lined the streets in Carthage, Africa as the parade of golden chariots made their way toward the city's mosque. The coffin of Hamilcar Barca was pulled by four well-trained horses dressed festively in gold barrettes. The horses strutted their stuff as if as though they were parading for a blue ribbon. After the parade reached the mosque, the long brigade parked their golden chariots at the base of the concrete steps and the Barca family was led in first.

Hamilcar Barca's body was openly displayed in his formal Carthaginian military uniform. His purple cape was draped fashionably across his broad shoulders and narrow waist. His widow and other family members were seated in

the front row of the mosque. Hannibal was joined
by Philip V of Macedonia. The two shook hands.

"Philip of Macedonia, it is so good to see
you again," Hannibal said to him.

"Hannibal, you have my most sincere
condolences," said Philip. "Your father was an
outstanding man and a true asset to this great
empire."

"Thank you, Philip," said Hannibal. "My
father has always considered you as his greatest
political and military ally."

"And an ally I was. I was vacationing in
Sparta when I received word of his passing. What
exactly happened?"

"According to the five assassins, the
Romans paid them 30 pieces of silver each to
assassinate my father. After my father was struck
by an arrow, another one was fired at me but our
military doctor caught the arrow instead."

"How is the doctor," asked Philip.

"He is live and recovering," answered Hannibal.

"Good, and yourself?"

"I am ready for war against Rome," Hannibal said.

"Listen, I have a large arsenal of weapons left over from the reign of my great-uncle, Alexander, the Great. Consider it yours. I am also sending ten thousand foot soldiers and thirty war ships to Rome with you. We Greeks also want to beat the Romans. Are there any other allied nations joining us in the war?"

"Yes," answered Hannibal. "All of Egypt, Ethiopia and Persia are sending troops. We also have ten thousand Zulus from the south accompanying us with five hundred elephants. Utica, Tyre and Babylon are also helping us with our weapons manufacturing. Philip, we mean business; big business!"

"Great! Let's do it," said Philip. "Let's beat Rome."

Giving the evening's eulogy was a Carthaginian minister. As he stood at the pulpit he spoke these words:

"Let us now begin. It is believed that when people see certain things as beautiful, something must become ugly. When people see certain things as good, something must become bad. Brightness relies on darkness, tallness defines shortness and the strong must always feed off the weak. Therefore, in our case, our freedom fighter has become another nation's terrorist. War, as we know it today and as it shall be known in the future, is nothing more than a balance of interest, and how you are directly affected by this interest depends upon your position within the apex of power."

After the eulogy and several testimonies, the members of the royal Barca family formed a receiving line on the balcony of the mosque. Thousands of people, with outstretched arms and waved hands, tried to get a glimpse of or gently touch the royal family's garments.

"Your father was greatly loved," Hanno said to Hannibal. "Look at all these people."

One by one, the royal members from other well-established nations waited in line to offer their condolences to the members of the Barca family.

"Ptolemy and my wife, Cleopatra, Pharaoh of Egypt. My deepest sympathy I offer to you all," he said in a bow. "May the spirit of Amen bless you all, always."

"May Allah be with you during these dark moments. Antiochus III, King of Syria," he said as he kissed the hand of Barca's widow.

"King Darius of Persia. May the sovereign God, Ahuramadza bless you with the kingdom of both heaven and earth," he said as his assistant handed each Barca member a special cut diamond.

Hannibal stepped toward the lectern and before the thousands of cheering spectators said:

"On behalf of the Barca Family, I want to thank each and every one of you for your generous support. Many of you are about to send your sons off to war for the very first time and despite their fears, we must go forward. Many of our allied nations don't speak the same language but we do share the same mission statement, and that is to beat the Romans. Now that I have been made chief in command of the Carthaginian army, I say onward to Rome and long live Carthage. Long live Carthage!"

"Long live Carthage," chanted the crowd. "Long live Carthage. Long live Carthage."

10

The Battle at Saguntum

The assassination of Carthage's chief military general was the beginning of the Second Punic War. The Carthaginians and their allied forces marched bodaciously northward toward the eastern town of Saguntum, Spain.

The appearance of the allied forces was both massive and overwhelming in both sight and sound. Thousands of chariots and hundreds of thousands of marching men and horses displayed a multi-cultural experience that was totally unfamiliar to the continent of Europe. Also unfamiliar to the continent of Europe were the monstrous beasts that accompanied Hannibal and his forces. These beasts, known as elephants, were mammoth in both size and weight. Thunderously, the elephants plodded fearlessly ahead and alongside the allied forces.

As the heat of the day wore on, swirling dust and biting winds made breathing conditions extremely difficult. Covered in dust from head to toe, many allied troops wore bandanas around their faces to protect themselves from the angered dust created by the chariots wheels and war animals.

Traveling five miles ahead of the allied forces was a Spanish scout and a Carthaginian drum communication officer. Their assignment was to scout out and communicate the unexpected.

"Look, over there," the Spanish scout said excitedly to his Carthaginian traveling companion. "An entire Roman fleet." They then hid themselves high in the hills.

"What is this location," asked the Carthaginian drummer.

"Saguntum," answered the Spanish scout.

"I must notify our armies," said the Carthaginian drummer. He transmitted his message by way of drum beats.

As Hannibal heard the sounds of the incoming drum beats, he signaled, with just a raise of his right hand, for the entire multi-cultural force to stop. Both men and animals obeyed his command. As he stood proudly in his golden chariot, he was approached by Hanno, his second in command.

"Sir, a large Roman infantry unit has just landed on the beaches of Saguntum," Hanno said.

"How many soldiers are there," Hannibal asked him.

Hanno signaled for his drummer to ask the question to the scouts ahead. Moments later he received an answer.

"Thirty-five thousand strong," Hanno said to Hannibal.

Hannibal turned toward his allied troops and said:

"First division, we'll take the point. Hasdrubal, you and the second division flank farther toward the right and move behind the hills. I want the Ethiopian sling throwers to remain behind the wall of elephants until I give the signal to start shooting. Hanno, you are in charge of the Greeks and the third division. Once the sling throwers have forced the Roman army into a huddled position, I want your division to parallel me in a V formation. Afterward, I want your elephants to box them in to prevent a retreat. Together, we shall encircle and crush them in their centered position. First division archers, cock, lock and let's get ready to roll. Everybody, forward march!"

A few miles ahead, the Roman army had unloaded their chariots, war animals and ammunition and had begun to travel southward toward the Carthaginian army. Within a matter of minutes, they were face to face with the Carthaginian forces. Both armies increased their trot and rode swiftly toward one another.

"Sling throwers, release arms," Hannibal commanded.

The sling throwers released hundreds of small iron pellets, via their sling shots, at the oncoming Roman army. As the bullet-like pellets showered down heavily on the Roman soldiers, they attempted to protect themselves with their shields.

"Second division, move out," Hannibal commanded from his swiftly moving chariot.

The second division broke from the ranks and disappeared behind the hills. Unnoticeably, they swiftly worked their way behind the Roman army.

"Form a huddle but continue to move forward," the Roman General said to his troops as he protected himself with his shield from the incoming pellets.

"Third division, parallel me in a V formation, now," Hannibal commanded.

The incoming pellets caused a great deal of confusion for the Roman army. As the pellets stung the horses, they reared up and shook the

Roman soldiers from their backs. A command was giving from the Roman general:

"Move the cavalry division forward, now!"

"We can't," returned another Roman officer.

"Why not?"

"Because our horses are too afraid of those huge beasts. They won't move beyond them. We're boxed in with no defense," said the Roman officer.

"Damn! We are about to get slaughtered," the general said with frustration.

Chaos swelled within the ranks of the Roman army. Besides getting hit with the iron pellets, the horses were spooked and continued to back away from the Carthaginian elephants.

As the elephants surrounded the boxed-in Roman unit, the Carthaginian javelin throwers, who were mounted high on the backs of elephants, released their javelins with fierce velocity.

Hundreds of javelins honed in on the Roman soldiers. The Romans quickly realized that their horses were too frightened to move forward. They dismounted from their horses and on foot, they charged toward the Carthaginians forces. A hand-to-hand combat commenced.

The members of Hannibal's point division sprang from their horses and chariots and immediately engaged in a sword fight with the Roman soldiers. To stabilize the situation many Roman archers took out many Carthaginian javelin throwers. The Carthaginian forces retaliated by releasing arrows, javelins and pellets.

On horseback, a Roman soldier charged toward Hannibal. As the horse rushed forward Hannibal picked up a spear, threw it at the Roman soldier and dove out of his way. The soldier was struck by the spear and fell hard onto the ground.

It took the Carthaginians and its allied troops two hours to defeat the Romans at Saguntum, Spain. Thousands of Carthaginians, Romans and allied troops lay deceased on the battle field. Pools of blood and its tainted scent, brought sickness to any weak stomach. Sick horses and wounded elephants wandered aimlessly around the corpses.

As Hannibal reviewed the aftermath of the onslaught, he was approached by Hasdrubal.

"Are you okay," Hannibal asked him.

"I have a few bumps and bruises but other than that, I'm fine," Hasdrubal answered. "What about yourself?"

"Likewise. It's nothing serious."

Both men were joined by Hanno.

"Sir, what do we do with our dead," Hanno asked Hannibal.

I want a head count of our wounded and our deceased. For our deceased, I want their bodies identified and a message sent to their families saying that they died bravely in battle," Hannibal said as he leaned on his chariot.

"Yes, sir," answered Hanno. He then began a head count of the wounded.

"Hannibal, I think that we need to give the men and animals a three-day rest before we move on," said Hasdrubal.

"I can go for that," Hannibal said. "Once we reach Barcelona, we'll take a three-day holiday. You know Hasdrubal, I really would like to invade Italy as soon as possible."

"How? After this defeat, the Romans will call to service every active man to guard all of their coastal borders."

"Exactly," Hannibal agreed. "What about their northern border?"

"France?"

"Yes, France," Hannibal answered. "They would never expect us to strike form the north. The Gauls from Germany would welcome our attack on Italy. Furthermore, the northern gate at Poppola, along Rome's Flaminia Way, is their most vulnerable entrance. I suggest that I move on to Rome while you keep open our communications and supply lines here in Spain."

"Great," Hasdrubal said.   "After the rest period, let's make it happen."

11

The Race to Marseilles

The Caracella bath house in Rome was a blend of assertive glass and gleaming brass. Sparked with a strong sculptural presence of Roman deities and a variety of solid geometric forms, the atmosphere offered more than just a simple bath; it was a way of life. Seasoned with a dash of arrogance, only Rome's elites were allowed to bathe behind these walls.

The towels were of the finest cotton from Egypt; the curtains were of the finest silks from Asia and the water was piped in hot from the clearest and healthiest lakes in the Alps mountains.

On this day, four of Rome's most prominent citizens were the bath house's guests for the evening. They were Fabius Maximus,

Cornelius Scipio, Aemilius Paullus and Terentius Varro. Both Paullus and Varro were senior officials within the Roman military.

"I'd like to make a toast to the New Roman Empire," said Fabius. "May it reign forever."

"To the Roman Empire," the other three said in a toast.

"To the beginning of Roman Renaissance, may its mark last forever on future civilizations," Cornelius said in a toast.

"To Roman Renaissance," the other three said in a toast.

A bath house waiter entered the room and whispered to Fabius. He then departed the room.

"Gentlemen, our scouting reporter has returned from Spain," said Fabius. "He has news concerning the Carthaginians."

A Roman scout reporter entered the steamy room with his helmet tucked underneath his arm.

He saluted Fabius and the other seated members and said:

"Sir, I am ashamed to report that the Carthaginians have destroyed our entire western Mediterranean infantry unit."

"The entire unit," Fabius asked loudly.

"Yes sir, the entire unit," answered the reporter.

Fabius threw a wet towel against the wall and asked with continued anger:

"Who is commanding the Carthaginian army?"

"General Barca's son, Hannibal," answered the reporter.

A second messenger entered the room. He, too, saluted Fabius and said:

"Sir, a message from Carthage, Africa."

"Read it," Fabius said with anger.

"To the Emperor Fabius Maximus and the members of the Roman Senate. Effective immediately, we, the governing body of Carthage, Africa, have chosen to cancel all war indemnity payments and all hidden slave trade agreements with Rome."

"That will ruin our economy," said Paullus.

"There's more," said the messenger. "We have also chosen to block all Roman ships traveling within the Mediterranean channel between Carthage and Sicily. All Roman citizens within the country will be arrested and expelled. This declaration of war comes to you with the full support of both our Greek and Arab allies. Signed, the King of Carthage."

"They can't be serious," Fabius replied.

"Oh yes, Fabius, they are serious and I'll tell you why," Cornelius said as he exited the bubbling water. "You see, the entire time that they were in Spain, they weren't just mining silver for trade and commerce. Oh no! They were preparing for war against us and this time, they won't stop until they reach Rome."

"Damn," shouted Fabius.

"Gentlemen, we are in deep, deep trouble," Cornelius said as he donned a dry towel.

"What do we do," asked Varro.

"We answer the call of war. That's what we'll do Varro," Cornelius said.

"Which means that I must go to the Italian people and ask them to again send their children back into war against Carthage," said Fabius.

"You really don't have much of a choice, Fabius," said Cornelius. "If you don't Rome will surely lie in ruins."

"Damn! I really didn't want this," Fabius said as he sat on a bench.

"But you must deal with it," Cornelius said as he sat next to Fabius. "Cheer up, gentlemen. There is hope. I'll go to war against this Hannibal. I beat his father in Sicily and I'll beat his son in Spain."

"Cornelius, I was there with you in Sicily," said Paullus. "We lost men at a four to one ratio against the Carthaginians. Sicily, Sardinia and Corsica were all costly wars and so will this one."

"Maybe, maybe not, Paullus," said Cornelius. "Right now, we are on the defense."

"So what are you proposing, Cornelius," asked Fabius. "After all, it was your idea to assassinate General Barca."

"This is my request. You give me fifty seven-thousand foot soldiers, five thousand cavalrymen and two hundred scouts and I'll crush this Hannibal within a week," said Cornelius.

"Sir, you'll need longer than a week," said the reporter. "Hannibal is lightning swift and he is as strong as his father. Actually, in my opinion, he's better."

"Really?" asked Cornelius.

"Really," answered the reporter. "I watched the entire battle of Saguntum from a hillside. I saw how swiftly and how cleverly the

Carthaginians segregated and slaughtered our troops. They where well trained and skillful."

"They always have been skillful," added Cornelius.

"Yes, but they have something we don't have," said the reporter. "A division of five hundred elephants."

"Elephants," Fabius asked looking shocked.

"Yes sir, elephants," answered the reporter.

"Hannibal's pugnacious tenacity is to be admired," said Cornelius.

"I might also add that the Carthaginians are able to track our every move in Spain by the use of drum communicating scouts. They know in advance how many soldiers we have and what direction we are moving in from," said the reporter.

"Interesting," said Fabius.

"Interesting indeed," said Cornelius. "Which is why I don't want to chance anything else. I say give me the troops and ammunition that I have requested and allow me to position myself along the French border. I'll land at Marseilles and there is where I'll defeat Hannibal."

"Why Marseilles, France," asked Varro.

"Because Varro, Hannibal is too confident in Spain and he has far too many allies," answered Cornelius. "Furthermore, he has colonized within the country and he knows the terrain extremely well. I think that its best to fight him on unfamiliar soil."

"I agree with Cornelius Scipio," said Fabius. "You have my blessings on obtaining the ammunition and the men you need to defeat Hannibal. We must warn the Italian people. We are officially at war with Carthage."

12

Brothers In Arms

The city of Barcelona, Spain was a small replica of Carthage, Africa. Many of its citizens indiscriminately enjoyed many of the same lavish perks that were available in Carthage. These perks were stately homes, great outdoor lawns and gardens, fine music, poetry and dining, and plenty of clean air and fresh water.

Also, synonymous to the city was the superb quality of racial harmony. Interaction between Carthaginians and Spaniards was a peaceful common practice. Mixed dating and marriages were allowed without social stress or conflict.

A traditional holiday for the Carthaginians was the feast day of Baal. Baal was the name of the Carthaginian's God. The name meant "owner" or "lord." Just as in early Palestine, the Carhaginians had a Baal for each locality and they had Baals or Baalim (plural) for objects such as rivers, desserts and mountains. The Baal of each locality was the local god of fertility and the people brought offerings to him in hope that he would make their crops grow and protect them in battle. Baal was the male element in creation, and his female counterpart was Astoreth or Astarte.

The feast day of Baal was celebrated in late November. Dining elegantly together and seated around a large dinner table were many leading families of Spain and the political and military leaders of Carthage. The evening's dinner began at five o'clock. It was hosted in a castle that overlooked the Mediterranean. Canvassed greens and yew hedges lined the walkway to the castle. As the guest poured into the diner room many were dressed in the sharpest garments of that era.

Hannibal, who was dressed in his traditional white silk turban and a loose-fitting pantsuit, was the last to enter the dining room. He and Leo, his pet lion, were escorted by the daughter of the

Spanish king. He took his seat at the table next to the king and waited for the music to stop.

The walls of the dining room were of pine with pearwood carvings. Above the archway entrance was a freshly carved inscription. The inscription read "Brothers in Arms."

The ebony dining table hosted a variety of meats and fowls. Accompanying the procession of food were spices and salad greens.

The king stood at the head of the table and signaled for the harps and lutes to cease playing. He then said:

"My brothers, it is an honor to dine with distinguished guests such as yourself. My country's wealth has increased tremendously due to our joint mining efforts. To celebrate the feast of Baal is also an honor. We, too, give thanks to Baal for the fine harvests, our new Carthaginian libraries, our stately homes and many other amenities that I am unable to think of at this moment. Our trading relationships with Carthage go way back and we have always had great relations. Please, from this day forward, may we always remain brothers in arms."

"Brothers in arms," everyone said to a toast.

"Now without further ado, lets eat," said the king.

Small talk and the sound of clanging silverware filled the dinner chamber. Many of the diners politely addressed one another and offered to pass certain dishes around the table.

"My, you have a strong appetite," the princess said to Hannibal.

"I must eat a lot. I have a strong libido."

"That could get you in a lot of trouble," she said.

"It hasn't yet. It has brought me nothing but pleasure."

"One day, I must share in your pleasure."

Hannibal then choked on his food.

High in the palace tower rooms the evening's vocal entertainers were rehearsing their skits. The framed-in-silence was broken by trills and musical scales of both Spanish and Carthaginian entertainers. Also filling the chambers were the tempos and acoustics in a space sixty feet tall.

After dinner the musical festivities had begun. Everyone present had a wonderful time singing along and dancing at the multi-cultural event. The ambience and the acoustics combined made the entire evening an uplifting experience.

Accompanying the chamber music were conversations among friends. As Hannibal strolled casually with the king's daughter fastened to his arm, he was joined by the king.

"Hannibal, have you enjoyed yourself this evening?"

"It was a wonderful evening and the music was just magnificent," said Hannibal.

"Good, good. So tell me Hannibal, how do you feel you will fare in history?"

"Well, as you know, all men don't share the same history. The history of Europe is not the history of Africa. Due to our own experiences, we interpret events differently. For instance, my war against Rome will be viewed by Europe as an unjust and barbaric event. Where, as we know, the truth is that this war is about retrieving what was wrongfully taken from Carthage, the islands. So how will I fare in history? It depends upon who tells the story and how the story is taught."

"Hannibal, you are a wise man and I will be proud to have you as my son-in-law," said the King. "May we always remain brothers in arms and may you always find peace in Baal, my brother."

"Peace in Baal, my brother."

13

A Boxed In Situation

At a campsite at Marseilles, France, Cornelius Scipio, Cnaeus Scipio, Aemilius Paullus and Terentius Varro were all dressed in battle armor. They stood around an outdoor table reviewing a map of Spain.

"Here is where we are. This is Marseilles," said Cnaeus Scipio. "Barcelona is southwest of here. I say, allow me to take our troops to Spain to drive Hannibal north into your hands."

"What if his resistance is too strong for you, Cnaeus. You'll need more troops," said Varro.

"Not really because we are going to box him in," said Cornelius. "Cnaeus will move in on

Hannibal from the south while I move in on him from the north. Varro, you and your troops will cut him off at the Mediterranean while you, Paullus, box him in on the west. All we need to do is to continue shrinking the box."

"I think that is a brilliant plan," said Paullus. "This way, Hannibal's drum communicators will keep his troops continuously mobile and unstable. Their communications will get fouled and so will their focus of attack."

"Exactly," agreed Cornelius. "It is the perfect boxed in situation."

All four men donned their helmets.

"I'm ready," said Cnaeus.

"Good. Let's do it," Cornelius said as he fastened his cape.

The four men divided and headed toward their troop section. Cnaeus was joined by his brother, Cornelius.

"You know Cornelius, this sounds like a brilliant plan but I have a bad feeling about this one," said Cnaeus.

"Yes, I know," said Cornelius. "There is a strange chill in the air."

Both men hugged each other.

"Good luck, my brother," Cnaeus said with teary eyes.

"Good luck."

14

Another One Bites the Dust

Quickly rolling in off the Mediterranean sea, over Barcelona, Spain were enormous black clouds. These clouds were accompanied by strong gusting winds and lightning. Periodically, the rumble of thunder would shake the sky.

Fast-moving storms were habitual for this part of Spain. As the high winds rushed inward toward Barcelona many of the area's trees and tall grasses bowed submissively in the direction of the storm.

Several miles south of Barcelona were the public growing fields of Tarragona. As Cnaeus Scipio and his troops raced toward the meadows, they were greeted by the field supervisor.

"Greeting," Cnaeus said to the field supervision.

"Greeting," returned the field supervision.

"We are looking for the army from Africa. Have you seen them?"

"Yes, they are beyond that hill."

"Thank you," Cnaeus said to him. He then turned toward his troops and said: "Let's move out. They are just over that hill."

Five miles west of Barcelona, Aemilius Paullus and his troops were scrambling in toward the city. As he listened to the sound of African drums he signaled for his troops to stop.

"Their military fort must be close by," Paullus said to his senior officer. "Let us form a v-shaped wall. I want the charioteers to strengthen the point and I want the cavalry to form and strengthen the outer wall. The infantry unit is to remain inside the formation until I give the word. Let's move out."

High on a hilltop, Hannibal, Hasdrubal and a Spanish guide observed Paullus and his troops form their broad v-shaped formation.

"What do you think," Hasdrubal asked Hannibal. "It looks like a strong formation to me."

"So does an outstretched chain," said Hannibal. "But a chain's greatest value can be found with its weakest link."

"Which means?"

"Which means that the weakest point of a v-formation is at its apex. If the point is not strongly enforced, it cannot penetrate. The whole formation will collapse in chaos. Come, let's prepare for battle."

All three men mounted their horses and headed back toward Barcelona.

Above, an indescribable black hue continued to swell over Barcelona. As the storm clouds increased in both strength and momentum many of the area's animals reacted with visible nervousness.

Terentius Varro and his troops had just landed at a beach east of Barcelona. He, too, heard the sounds of African drums. With his red cape blowing furiously in the wind, he wrapped it around himself and said to his troops:

"Present arms. Form a line and continue to move forward."

After Hannibal, Hasdrubal and the Spanish guide had ridden back into Barcelona, they were greeted by a breathless drum scout.

"Sir, Roman soldiers are everywhere. They are to the north, south, east and west of us. It appears that we are boxed in."

Hannibal was joined by several other Carthaginian and allied officers. He placed a map of the area on a table and drew a box around Barcelona. He drew four arrows that pointed toward each corner of the box. He then said:

"The Romans are here, here, here and here. Now this is the plan. I want each of our four elephant tank divisions to strike only at the corners of the Roman box formation. Once penetration has been achieved, I want our Greek forces to rush forward toward the corners and surround the outside perimeters of the box. I don't want you to attack the Romans, just position yourself. Give me about forty minutes of battle before you move in. I want to tire the Romans out before you strike. So, while we're fighting the box from the inside, our allied forces will be fighting it from the outside. As the battle continues, the Roman box formation should deteriorate. Got it?"

"Got it," answered the surrounding officers.

"Good. Hanno, I want every elephant given plenty of rice wine. I want them juiced up and crazed with anger."

"Yes, sir," answered Hanno.

"All right, my brothers, let's take it to them."

Within a matter of minutes the Roman army had formed their box formation around the city of Barcelona. Cornelius Scipio rode out onto the battle field to address the Carthaginians and their allied forces. Hannibal, in his chariot, rode out chivalrously to meet him.

"So, you are the infamous Hannibal Barca," Cornelius said to him.

"Hannibal Barca, yes. Infamous, no."

"Hannibal, you do realize that I have you boxed in. Furthermore, I am twenty-five years' your senior."

"Old fools die young."

"If I were you, I would let go of that vain African pride and spare these men their lives."

"For starters, you are not me. Secondly, allow me to define a Carthaginian. Being a Carthaginian is more than just being an African; it is the exclamation of our attitude. We, Carthaginians, gave Rome its culture, its architecture and its political system. We even shared a portion of our trade routes and rich harvest fields with you in Sicily, Corsica and Sardinia but no, this wasn't good enough. You wanted it all. So, just being a Carthaginian gives me the right to be vain."

Both men gave each other a long, hard stare.

"So be it. If war with Rome is what you want, then war with Rome is what you'll get," Cornelius said to him. Both leaders returned to their battle field positions.

Above, stronger winds and darkening skies continued. The sky developed a night time appearance.

"Well how did it go," a Roman officer asked Cornelius.

"Prepare to charge. We are going to war," Cornelius said.

"Is everyone ready," Hannibal asked Hasdrubal.

"They are ready," he answered.

"Great. Let's make it happen. Charge," Hannibal commanded to his troops.

That moment lightening struck and rain poured profusely.

All four Roman infantries, cavalry and chariot divisions rushed down the hills around Barcelona. Below, the Carthaginian elephants scrambled toward the corners of the box formation. As anticipated, the elephants broke through the Roman lines.

In the wet knee-high grass both armies' cavalry units were the first to make physical contact. Several Carthaginian soldiers dove from their horses and onto Roman cavalrymen. After they hit the ground another physical encounter had begun.

As the Roman chariots came within striking distance of the Cargthaginian chariots both sides' archers released their arrows. Both armies had encountered severe losses from the arrows. After many charioteers were struck, their speeding chariots overturned and tumbled several times before they came to rest on their top sides. Their injured horses wobbled to their feet.

As they sprinted through the high grass, the Carthaginian javelin throwers released their spears. Many Roman soldiers were struck. The Roman archers released more arrows from their charging chariots. More Carthaginians were struck and fell hard from their chariots. Those unable to fall free from their chariots were dragged along the wet bumpy terrain by their runaway chariots.

Both sides foot soldiers met face to face. They immediately started their wrestling matches and sword fights. A runaway Carthaginian chariot crashed into a crowd of battling soldiers.

As the elephants continued to break through the line of Roman soldiers, many were trampled. Carthaginian javelin throwers and Ethiopian sling throwers released their ammunition, from covered platforms, mounted high on the elephants' backs.

As planned, the Greek allied troops ran alongside the Carthaginian elephants. They hurdled over many fallen Roman soldiers. Once they reached the outside perimeter, with cocked bows, they formed a surrounding wall around the Romans and assumed an attack position.

The heavy rains created poor visibility for both armies. Cursed with darkening skies, heavy winds and swiftly dropping temperatures, two of the Roman leaders gathered for a brief conference.

"Paullus, I think we're in trouble," said Varro.

"What do you mean?"

"It looks as if as though Hannibal has reversed his position against us."

Paullus shoved an Ethiopian soldier toward the ground and observed the Greeks in their poised position. He then said to Varro:

"Hmmmmm! Now this is a bad situation."

"And it's going to get even worse," said Varro. "Look all around us. Hannibal's allied forces have us surrounded."

"And they are not striking."

"Of course not. He's attempting to tire us out. This is going to be a massacre. With the quickness, we should get the hell out of here, now!"

"Really," Paullus agreed. "To hell with this. The Carthaginians can have Spain. Let's call a retreat."

"What about the brothers Scipio?"

"I don't know where they are. Hopefully, they will recognize our bad situation and follow us in a retreat. We can't win in this situation."

"No, we can't. I'm out of here. I'll meet you in Rome," said Varro.

"Good luck," said Paullus.

"Good luck."

Both men climbed into an empty chariot and shouted to their men:

"Retreat! Follow me."

Hannibal recognized the Romans attempting a retreat. He then gave the command to the Greek forces:

"Allied forces, fire!"

The Greeks released hundreds of arrows at the fleeing Roman army. Many Roman soldiers fell victim to the reversed boxed in formation.

This battle lasted for twelve hours. Many Roman, Greek and Carthaginian soldiers lay deceased on the battle field. Above, a clear sky had returned.

Hannibal greeted Hasdrubal with a strong forearm hand shake. Both men were covered with mud from head to toe.

"Well, another one bites the dust," Hannibal said.

"Yes, another one bites the dust," Hasdrubal said in return. "Your plan worked beautifully. My congratulations on a job well done."

"Thank you, my brother. I see that we didn't lose nearly as many as the Romans. I suspect that for every one we lost, they lost four."

"I'd say so. So what now," Hasdrubal asked him.

Both men walked together.

"We move according to plan. Tomorrow I'm heading for Italy by way of France. I want you to guard Spain against the Romans. Can you do it?"

"No problem. Hey, isn't he the Roman General whom you met before the battle?"

Both Scipio brothers lay dead next to one another.

"Yes it is and that's his brother next to him," Hannibal said. "Once again, another one bites the dust."

Crossing the Alps

The snow-capped panoramic view of the
Appenines mountains, in southern France was a
sight unseen before by the Carthaginians and their
allied troops. The symmetrical elevations of the
mountains, combined with high powered winds and
sub-zero temperatures, made scaling the mountains
a dare for only the brave.

Spewing down the sides of the octagonal
shaped mountains were large slabs of ice. This
spewed ice also glazed the narrow canyon that led
through the mountains. As the forty-mile-an-hour
winds blew through the canyon they echoed like
howling wolves. Pointed ice sickles hung like
daggers and tree ornaments from the cliffs above.
Blanketing the path ahead were miles and miles of
virgin snow.

"These are the Appenines Mountains," the Spanish guide said to Hannibal. "On the other side is northern Italy."

"How long will it take us to cross over these mountains," Hannibal asked him.

"It is hard to say, Senor. Winter has come early this year. The passage ways are narrow and icy. You may want to consider wintering here in France until spring. By then, a great deal of the snow and ice would have melted away."

"No, spring is too late," said Hannibal. "We must go now."

"Si, Senor, but I must advise you that you will loose many of your elephants due to the cold and narrow cliffs."

"I can handle losing a few elephants better than I can an entire nation. Let's go," Hannibal commanded.

The Carthaginians and their allied troops trekked up the snow-covered mountain. Midway up, along a narrow and icy passage way, several defiant elephants refused to go any farther. A Carthaginian herdsman tried to encourage them along.

"Balla! Balla," said the herdsman.

The elephants still refused to move.

"What is the problem," Hannibal asked the herdsman.

"The elephants are refusing to go forward. They are afraid of the height."

Above, the Appenines' hill people began dropping large boulders on the Carthaginian expedition team. Many of the large boulders missed but tumbled deep into the canyon below.

"Everyone, remain calm," Hannibal said. "Light some torches and begin melting away some of the ice. Archers, fire several rounds of arrows at those hicks above."

Hannibal and several of his soldiers lit torches and dragged them along the icy passage way. Hanno, his assistant, carefully edged his way toward Hannibal.

"Hannibal, we must find a place to make camp," he said. "This hawk (i.e., cold and windy weather) is too much to handle. I've never felt this kind of weather before."

"Snow is new to all of us," said Hannibal.

"Senor Hannibal, you must calm down your elephants or they'll create an avalanche," said the Spanish guide.

"What is an avalanche," Hannibal asked him.

"That is when huge slabs of snow come crashing down on us," said the guide. "Stomping and loud noise usually creates one."

"Hanno, calm those elephants down and get me some rope," Hannibal ordered.

"What are you going to do," Hanno asked as he handed Hannibal the rope.

"I am going to make a rope-like guard-rail for everyone to hold on to."   "Archimedes," he called.

"Sir," answered Archimedes.

"Pass the word. I want all three divisions to stretch out and tie ropes between divisions. I then want the ropes fastened to the walls at six foot intervals."

The defiant elephants began to panic again Many of them tried to run but stumbled and fell over the cliff's icy edge. The remaining elephants panicked even more.

"Senor, please calm the elephants," the guide begged Hannibal.

"Abdul, I don't want to die on foreign soil. Calm those elephants down, now," Hannibal ordered.

Abdul managed to calm down the elephants. Afterward, they edge easily along the icy cliff. By the end of the day, the guide had led the

Carthaginians and their allied troops to a flat field within the mountains. He then said to Hannibal:

"There are several caves just ahead. We can make camp there for tonight."

"All right, let's go," Hannibal said.

As both men leaped forward, they disappeared underneath a collapsed floor of snow. The mountain began to quake all around the expedition team. It was then followed by a huge roar.

"It's an avalanche. Everyone head for the caves," shouted another Spanish guide.

All around them large slabs of snow and ice broke free from their setting. As the snow rushed down the mountainsides it flattened trees and other debris that were within its path.

The entire Carthaginian allied force, along with their elephants, horses and oxen, all made a run for the caves ahead. Hanno began searching for Hannibal and the Spanish guide. He looked down into the collapsed hole but did not see either

Hannibal or his guide. He immediately noticed that Hannibal's rope had continued to feed into the hole. He grabbed part of the rope, formed a lasso and threw it around a fast-moving horse. He then ran alongside the horse, mounted it and steered it toward the cave's entrance.

Hannibal and the guide were pulled out of the hole and dragged along the snow covered terrain. Both men held onto the rope as Hanno raced against a ten-foot wall of snow and ice. Once Hanno safely entered the cave, a ten-foot wall of snow slammed heavily into another wall of snow. Hannibal and the guide were helped to their feet.

"Damn, that was fun," Hannibal said. "Hanno, you were right. We need to make camp immediately." He then released a roar of a laugh.

His troops joined him in laughter.

16

An Enemy from Within

"Damn! Damn! I am having buzzard luck against these Carthaginians," shouted Fabius. "You mean to tell me that both Cornelius and Cnaeus Scipio are dead?"

"Yes, sir," answered both Paullus and Varro.

Fabius threw his dinner plate against a wall. He, along with several other Roman senators, were dining together. He the asked both men:

"Why weren't the two of you killed?"

"Because it didn't take us long to interpret the situation," answered Varro. "You must speak with Philip of Macedonia to work out some kind of treaty. We don't have enough men in all of Italy to fight both the Greeks and the Carthaginians."

"Fabius, you must listen to us," said Paullus. "Hannibal has all of north Africa and half of the Arab world fighting with him as well. I'm telling you, He means business."

"And I don't," Fabius asked sarcastically. "I'm not just sitting here writing poetry, gentlemen. What else can we do?"

"Excuse me, sir, but I know how to beat the Carthaginians," said a young man at the end of the dinner table.

"And who are you," Fabius asked him.

"Publius Scipio," answered the young man. "It was my father, Cornelius, who was killed in Spain."

"Come forward," Fabius said to the young man.

Publius left his seat and approached Fabius.

"My, you are the young aedile Cornelius left in charge of public works," said Fabius. "No son, I can't let you go into battle against a well-trained Carthaginian army."

"And the Greeks," added Paullus.

"But sir, I know how to defeat the Carthaginians," Publius insisted.

"He's just a boy," said a seated senator. "Get him out of here."

"Wait! Let us hear the young man out," said Fabius. "We can use some fresh ideas around here. Son, what is your plan?"

"Well for starters, we have been fighting the Carthaginians incorrectly. In order to produce an apple, you need another apple. To give birth to a Roman, you need to mate with a Roman. Therefore, in order to beat a Carthaginian, you need another Carthaginian."

"And do you have such a person who would go against his own country," Fabius asked him.

"Indeed I do."

Small talk began around the table.

"Silence," said Fabius. "Who is this person?"

"He is an old friend of my father. Together, they ran the largest slave trade north of the Mediterranean. He is Sheik Massinissa, of north Africa."

"Is this Sheik Massinissa a Carthaginian, himself," asked Fabius.

"Yes he is," answered Publius. "And he can get our troops beyond the great wall of Carthage."

"Why? Why would a Carthaginian allow himself to become an enemy from within," asked Fabius. "Is this some kind of trick?"

"To the contrary," answered Publius. "It is not a trick. The King of Carthage has not only taken away his right to trade slaves but he has also confiscated all of his slaves. Those were his slaves who excavated the silver mines in Spain."

"So this man seeks revenge against his own country?"

"This is what he is proposing," said Publius. "If he can get us into Carthage and once we have captured the city, he wants the monopoly on the Carthaginians who are converted into slaves."

"And if we fail?"

"He wants protection as a Roman citizen," answered Publius.

"At this point, I'm desperate. That sounds like a fair trade to me. Senators, this is what I am proposing. I would like to send Publius Scipio to Carthage with five thousand specially trained soldiers. Son, is there anything else I can offer you?"

"Yes sir. I would like your permission to go to southern Spain before we move onto Carthage."

"Why," asked Fabius.

"Sheik Massinissa suggests that we cut off and destroy the Carthaginian communications and supply lines. He knows where every drum communicator is positioned. Once we rid the Carthaginians of their drum communicators, they'll no longer know how to prepare themselves for war against us."

"Good idea," said Fabius. "Senators, this dinner is over. Let's go get Carthage!"

17

Off With his Head

On a cool and breezy night in Barcelona, Spain Hasdrubal and several other Greek and allied officers sat in front of an outdoor fire. In front of the fire, on a large table, they played a game similar to dominos.

Publius Scipio and Sheik Massinissa were hidden on a hillside that overlooked the peaceful setting.

"The first drum communicator is on top of that hill," said Sheik Massinissa. "His job is to warn the camp of any nearby intruders. Usually, the second drummer is about a half mile away. Beyond that, they are spread out at one-mile intervals."

"In case they begin signaling to one another, can you interpret their messages," Publius asked him.

"Of course. I am a Carthaginian."

"Good," said Publius. "This is what I want. I want to take out all drum communicators within a five-mile radius of the city. I also want to take out the leader and only the leader. Can you point him out to me?"

"Yes. There he is. He is Hannibal's brother-in-law, Hasdrubal.

"Great. When everyone's fast asleep, we will tip in and grab him" said Publius.

After five hours of dominos Hasdrubal decided to call it quits. The time was well beyond midnight.

"My brothers, I am retiring for the evening," he said. "As usual, it has been a pleasure but I am tired of beating you all."

"We'll get you next time," said a Greek officer.

"If there is a next time," said Hasdrubal. "Good night, gentlemen."

Publius Scipio and Sheik Massinissa waited until Hasdrubal returned to his quarters. Publius then leaned over toward his officers and said:

"I want five of you to go with Sheik Massinissa. He will instruct you about what needs to be done. The remaining five, come with me."

At a lookout point that overlooked Barcelona, a Carthaginian drum scout sat quietly at his post. After he nodded off for sleep for the third time, he was quietly attacked by Sheik Massinissa and three Roman soldiers.

At a second lookout position, another drum scout was eating a piece of fruit. He heard a noise. He withdrew his sword and carefully inspected the area around him. He found nothing. Afterward, he returned to his post. From behind, he too, was quietly attacked by Sheik Massinissa and three Roman soldiers.

After he took out several Carthaginian drum scouts, Sheik Massissina rejoined Publius Scipio on the hillside. He then said to Publius:

"It's done. We've knocked out every drum communicator within five miles of the city."

"Excellent," said Publius. "Archers, take your position. Do not fire any arrows unless its necessary. This is not a war but a covert kidnaping. Massinissa, please wait here. The rest of you come with me."

Publius and a small band of Roman soldiers quietly slipped into Barcelona. As they took cover behind buildings and large trees they worked their way toward Hasdrubal's bungalow. They immediately rushed in.

An on-duty Carthaginian sentry noticed that Hasdrubal's door was opened. As he walked toward Hasdrubal's bungalow he was struck in the back with an arrow from a Roman archer seated high on a hillside.

Hasdrubal was dragged out of his bungalow. His mouth was gagged and both of his arms were tied together.

Another Carthaginian sentry spotted Hasdrubal being dragged off. As he attempted to sound the alarm, he too, received an arrow from a Roman archer.

Hasdrubal was rushed out of town and up a steep hillside. His body was thrown across a horse. He then recognized Sheik Massinissa. He forced the gag from his mouth and said to him:

"Why Massinissa? Is money that important to you? Where is your love for Carthage?"

"I lost it when they took away my slaves," answered Sheik Massinissa. Take him away and off with his head."

18

The Battle at Cannae

The view that overlooked northern Italy was well-welcomed by Hannibal and his allied troops. Spring had arrived. The spacious green prairies below offered a softer, warmer and a sunnier climate. Across the Po River, deep within its valley, were tall grasses, fresh meadow brooks and soft colored lilies that swayed gently in the wind.

Many of Hannibal's troops and war animals were in reasonably good shape. The climatic challenges that had once faced them were now well behind them.

Hannibal put his arm around Christo, his Spanish guide and said:

"Christo, you have done well." He then mounted his horse and said to his troops: "Saddle up, boys. Next stop, Rome."

Paullus and Varro were seated together in the Parthenon that overlooked Cannae, Italy. They, along with two other high-ranking Roman senators, were having a casual conversation and were enjoying a bottle of Italian wine.

"Whose turn is it to command the army today," asked a senator.

"Mine," answered Varro.

"Do you think that a unit of forty thousand troops can protect mother Italy," asked the second senator.

"Of course," answered Varro. "The Carthaginians couldn't possibly attack us in Italy. All of our waterfront borders are sealed off."

They then felt a quake followed by a continued rumble.

"What is that," asked the first senator.

"I don't know," answered the second senator. "It sounds like thunder to me."

"There is not a cloud in the sky," said Paullus.

"You're right," said Varro. "There isn't a single cloud above. As a matter of fact, it sounds more like a huge, fast-moving army."

All four men stopped and stared at one another.

"It couldn't be," said Varro. "This is Cannae, Italy.

"It couldn't be what," asked the first senator.

"Carthaginians," said Varro. He dropped his cup of wine, ran toward his chariot and rode off toward the edge of the Acropolis. He was joined by Paullus and the two senators.

Below, Hannibal and his fast-moving army were headed directly toward the Acropolis.

"What the ... How could this be," Paullus asked with amazement. "They are right at our doorstep."

"No; they are not at our doorstep," said the first senator. "They are in the house."

"How could they have possibly made their way into Italy," Varro asked himself.

"The Alps," suggested the second senator.

All three men gave the second senator a puzzled look,

"Think about it," said the second senator. "If all of our waterfront borders were sealed off and Hannibal knew it, France, and over the Alps, was his only way in. This Hannibal is a brilliant general. His father has taught him well."

"Italy is in trouble now," said Varro. "Sound the alarm. We are back at war."

As the Carthaginians raced towards the Acropolis their army was composed of four thousand cavalrymen at the point, eight hundred charioteers flanked both sides of the point and twenty elephants flanked both chariot divisions. Running swiftly behind the enclosed oblong shaped unit were fifteen thousand infantrymen. Hannibal led the charge on horseback.

The Roman army rode out from the Acropolis to meet the Carthaginians. They were forty thousand strong. Both Paullus and Varro led the charge.

As the two armies came together, the charioteers and the elephants swiftly split and quickly created a balloon-shaped formation. Once the Roman army was in the well of the formation, the elephants, which were again crazed with rice wine, came together and split the Roman army in half. The Romans were now sectioned off and the entire army was forced to fight with the Aufidius river at their back. This created poor mobility for the Romans. They were now no longer able to fight for Italy, but only for their lives.

The Roman archers stopped in front of the river and took a kneeling position. They cocked their bows and waited for the firing command. Paullus gave the command:

"Fire!"

The archers released their arrows. They struck many of the allied forces, but not enough to stop the continued push into the river.

The Ethiopian sling throwers loaded their slings and released their pellets at the Roman archers. Many archers were no longer able to withstand the constant influx of pellets. They quickly broke from the ranks and began fighting singlehandedly against the Carthaginians.

The Carthaginian javelin throwers released their spears. Many Roman cavalrymen were knocked off their horses. Those who did not die immediately, received a painful jab from an allied trooper's sword.

A Carthaginian charioteer was struck by a Roman arrow. The chariot lost control and flipped over several times. The tumbling chariot rolled in the way of a Carthaginian cavalry rider. The rider tried to hurdle the tumbling chariot but was unsuccessful. He, and his horse, tumbled head first into the dirt.

Hannibal and Paullus had engaged in a sword fight from horseback. Paullus scooped up a large stone and threw it at Hannibal. The stone struck Hannibal in his left eye. This permanently robbed him of his eye sight in that particular eye. As the blood spewed down Hannibal's face he continued the fight with Paullus.

Varro's horse accidentally backed into Hannibal's horse. Hannibal reacted to the intrusion with a blow to Varro's skull. Varro leaped from his horse and avoided the blow entirely. He then mounted a freestanding horse and rode off.

Hannibal and Paullus continued their sword fight. Paullus cleverly knocked Hannibal's sword out of his hand. He then smiled at Hannibal. Hannibal reached into his boot and withdrew a small dagger. He threw it at Paullus. The dagger struck Paullus in the throat. Paullus clutched his throat and then fell dead toward the ground.

After four hours of battle, many of the Romans were either dead or waiting in the river. The Aufidius river, which was once blue, ran red with blood for an entire week. The entire Roman army had been slaughtered. The poor mobility was a guaranteed win for Hannibal.

Varro's tiring horse wobbled to the top of the Acropolis. He dismounted his horse and watched how unmercifully the Carthaginians and their allied troops slaughtered the wounded Roman soldiers in the river. He then entered a fresh chariot and rode off to Rome.

A Rude Finding

On the steps of the Roman Senate, Fabius gave a call-to-arms-speech to not only the Latins, but to the Italian people as well.

"People, I can assure you that this war with Carthage will not be long lived," he said. "I need to recruit more men to guard our borders." His speech was interrupted as Varro rode up toward the steps. "What now," he asked Varro.

"The Carthaginians are in Italy," Varro said. "We were just annihilated in Cannae."

Chaos erupted. Loud screams and wailing filled the city as the Italian people stampeded for shelter. The old and injured were trampled as the helter-skelter activity became widespread. The senators shouted hysterically at Fabius.

"This is your fault, Fabius," said a senator. "You promised us that this wouldn't happen."

"Silence. I'm still Emperor here!"

"Not for long, said another senator. "Hannibal's at the gate.

"You watch your mouth," Fabius said to the senator. "Varro, how many did we loose at Cannae?"

"At least forty thousand," he answered.

"And Paullus," he asked.

"He's dead."

"So what are you going to do now, Fabius; write poetry," asked another senator.

"You should watch you mouth, Pal."

"So what are you going to do? Feed me to the Carthaginians," asked the senator.

"Gentlemen, gentlemen. This is exactly what the Carthaginians want us to do," said Varro. "To begin arguing and fighting amongst ourselves. I suggest that we maintain a level head and decide our next immediate defense. The Carthaginians are less than thirty miles away."

"You're right. I'm sorry," the senator said to Fabius.

"Varro, what is our weakness against Hannibal," Fabius asked.

"His long range weaponry," he said. He handed Fabius a small pellet. "These small metal pellets can travel three times as far as our conventional arrows. These pellets are released from cowhide slings. A skillful slinger can hit a tree at a distance of three hundred yards."

Fabius carefully reviewed the pellet. He then said:

"It has extremely sharp edges."

"And they heat up during flight," said Varro. "That is what make them so dangerous. Upon impact, they burn and once inside the flesh, they rip your insides."

"At this point, there is only one way to defeat Hannibal," said Fabius. "He is on a winning streak and his confidence is extremely high. We must beat him mentally. How did he get into Italy?"

"I suspect that he came in over the French Alps," answered Varro.

"You see, to move an army his size, over and across the cold French Alps, required a large amount of self confidence," said Fabius. "We must upset his rhythm with a rude finding."

"I've got just the thing," shouted Publius Scipio. He and Sheik Massinissa rode up, in their chariot, toward Fabius. From a sack Publius withdrew the head of Hasdrubal.

An awed sound came from the senators.

"Publius, what is that," Fabius asked him.

"It is the rude finding you just spoke of. It is the cut off head of Hannibal's brother-in-law, Hasdrubal."

"Son, your methods are somewhat barbaric but I do like them," said Fabius. "Find me a night rider."

Hannibal's at the Gate

All was calm within the Carthaginian campsite in Italy. Both the Carthaginians and their allied forces were fast asleep in the high grass. Just on the outside perimeter of the camp was a sleepy allied sentry. His responsibilities were to keep watch over the campsite. He was wedged between two large boulders.

Climbing on top of the two boulders was Publius Scipio and two Roman soldiers. Once Publius made it to the top of the boulder he whispered to the sleepy sentry:

"Hey, catch!"

He tossed to him the cut off head of Hasdrubal. Afterward, they quickly fled from the scene.

After the sentry caught the head, he dropped it in horror and ran hysterically into the camp.

Hannibal heard the scream, jumped out of his cot and dashed out of his tent. He and other soldiers wrestled the hysterical sentry to the ground. The screaming sentry then pointed at the head of Hasdrubal.

Hannibal picked up the head, recognized it and said nothing. He let go a sigh and said to the surrounding soldiers:

"It's Hasdrubal. The Romans have killed him."

"I guess the drum messages were true," said Hanno. "The Romans did kidnap him with the intent to kill him."

"And Massinissa is working with the Romans," added Archimedes.

"Massinissa has always been a greedy man," said Hanno. "He thinks only of himself."

"With teary eyes and Hasdrubal's head in his arms, Hannibal walked away from the soldiers. He walked over toward a shovel and dug a hole. He then placed the head into the small grave and covered it with dirt. Afterward, he walked into his tent. Moments later, he exited dressed for battle. He then began walking toward Rome.

"Hannibal, don't do it," said Hanno. "You always taught us to think rationally rather than emotionally. Isn't that how we won our battles?"

Hannibal said nothing. He continued to walk toward Rome.

"Hannibal, please listen to Hanno," said Archimedes. "There are more than fifty thousand soldiers guarding the gates of Rome. Our troops need more time to rest and replenish their strength.

Hannibal stopped to observe the cattle resting in the pasture. He looked at the lantern that Archimedes was holding. He then said:

"Then we shall remove the soldiers from the gate."

"How," asked Hanno.

"I want you to round up every available lantern," said Hannibal. I also want you to round up every head of cattle we have."

"Why," asked Hanno.

"Because we are going to tie the lanterns to the horns of the cattle and stampede them off into the hills that surround Rome," said Hannibal. "The Roman troops will rally and chase after the cattle, thinking that we are storming the hills."

"Thereby leaving the gate poorly guarded," added Archimedes.

"Exactly," said Hannibal. "Let's get busy."

Within an hour, the heads of five hundred cattle were dressed with lit lanterns. Hannibal dressed only half of his men for battle. He allowed the others to rest. He then said to twenty of his herdsmen:

"I want you to stampede the cattle east of Rome. Once the Romans have discovered that they were just chasing cattle, I want you all to take cover; don't risk your lives. Is that understood?"

"Yes sir," answered the head herdsman.

"Good, the rest of you come with me," said Hannibal.

The twenty herdsmen stampeded the cattle on the eastern hills of Rome. As anticipated, the fifty thousand Italian troops rallied and chased after the light-bearing animals.

Once the coast was clear, Hannibal and his troops quickly raced down toward the gates of Rome. A Roman sentry spotted Hannibal and the Carthaginians and yelled:

"Hannibal's at the gate. Hannibal's at the gate."

This small scuffle was another embarrassing loss for the Romans. Thousands of lives were lost that starlit night just outside the city. After that particular battle, Hannibal conquered a great deal of Italy and controlled it for well over fifteen years. Fabius was ousted as emperor and Varro and Publius Scipio, who was later called Africanus, took command of Italy. In 201 B.C., Rome made peace with Carthage. Spain was returned to it original sovereignty.

This story was a modern interpretation of a particular event in history. It was the story of Hannibal, the ultimate warrior.

The End.

Don't miss the continuing saga:

Hannibal:
The Final Battle: Bad to the Bone

and these other novels by Joseph Peebles:

Tuscaloosa:
A True Choctaw Chief
(The Hernando De Soto Chronicles)

and

The Adventures of
New Jack Swing
(A Spy Novel)

BIBLIOGRAPHY

Johnson, J.L. The Black Biblical Heritage (Winston-Derek Publishers, Inc., 1993).

Lazenby, J.F. Hannibal's War: a Military History of the Second Punic War (Aris & Phillips, 1978).

Roger, J.A. World's Great Men of Color (Collier MacMillian Publishers, 1972).

Nash-Williams, A.H., editor. Hannibal Triumphant: Selections from Nepos and Livy (St. Martin's Press, 1969).

Jochannan, Yosef ben- and Henrick Clark, John. New Dimensions in African History (African World Press, Inc., 1991)

Grant, Michael. History of Rome (Scribner's, 1978).

Setton, K.M. The Renaissance: Maker of Modern Man (National Geographic, 1970).

BIBLIOGRAPHY